CONTENTS

ALEXANDER-GRACE EDUCATION

Understanding the MAP Tests

The NWEA MAP (Measures of Academic Progress) test is an adaptive assessment that is designed to measure student growth and progress in a variety of subject areas. The test is taken by millions of students across the United States and is widely used by educators to help inform instruction and measure student outcomes. The NWEA MAP test is administered online and provides immediate feedback on student performance, allowing teachers to adjust their teaching strategies and provide targeted support to individual students.

The NWEA MAP test is unique in that it is adaptive, which means that the difficulty of the questions adjusts based on the student's responses. This allows the test to be more personalized to each student's abilities and provides a more accurate measure of their knowledge and skills. The test covers a range of subject areas, including mathematics, reading, language usage, and science, and is administered multiple times throughout the school year. This allows teachers to track student progress and growth over time and make data-driven decisions to improve student outcomes.

Purpose and Benefits of MAP Testing

The primary purpose of the MAP Test is to provide valuable insights into a student's learning and academic progress. By offering a detailed analysis of a student's performance in reading, language usage, mathematics, and science, the test helps teachers tailor their instruction to meet individual needs. The MAP Test also serves as a benchmarking tool, allowing schools and districts to compare their students' performance with national norms and other local institutions.

This data-driven approach enables educators to make informed decisions about curriculum, instructional methods, and resource allocation, ultimately leading to improved student outcomes. Additionally, the MAP Test can help identify gifted students who may benefit from advanced or accelerated programs, as well as students who may require additional support or interventions.

Test Format and Content

The MAP Test is divided into four primary content areas: reading, language usage, mathematics, and science. Each section consists of multiple-choice questions that cover various topics and skills within the respective subject. The test is untimed, allowing students to work at their own pace and ensuring a lower level of test anxiety. The computer-adaptive nature of the MAP Test ensures that the difficulty of questions adjusts based on a student's performance, making it suitable for students of all ability levels. As a result, the MAP Test not only evaluates a student's mastery of grade-level content but also assesses their readiness for more advanced material.

Adaptive Testing and Scoring System

One of the unique aspects of the MAP Test is its adaptive testing system. As students answer questions, the test adjusts the difficulty of subsequent questions based on their performance. This adaptive nature allows the test to home in on a student's true ability level, providing more accurate and meaningful results. The MAP Test uses a RIT (Rasch Unit) scale to measure student achievement, which is an equal-interval scale that allows for easy comparison of scores across grade levels and subjects. This scoring system allows educators and parents to track a student's growth over time, making it an invaluable tool for understanding academic progress and setting individualized learning goals.

Preparing for Success on the MAP Test

Effective preparation for the MAP Test involves a combination of understanding the test format, mastering content knowledge, and developing test-taking strategies. This test prep book is designed to provide students with comprehensive guidance on each content area, offering targeted instruction and practice questions to build confidence and ensure success. Additionally, the book includes test-taking tips and strategies to help students approach the test with a calm and focused mindset. By working through this book and dedicating time to consistent practice, students will be well-equipped to excel on the MAP Test and achieve their academic goals.

Note that, since there is no cap to the level that a student can work to in preparation for this test, there is no 'completion' of content, as students can simply do questions from grades above in preparation. It should be noted that students are not expected to work far above grade level to succeed in this test, as consistent correct answers are more relevant.

What Is Contained Within this Book?

Within this book you will find 320 questions based off content which would be found within the MAP test your student will take. The content found in this book will be the equivalent of grade 4 level. Note that since this test is adaptive, some students may benefit by looking at several grade levels of content, not just their own.

At the end of the book will contain answers alongside explanations. It is recommended to look and check your answers thoroughly in regular intervals to make sure you improve as similar questions come up.

Number	Topic Name	Questions	Answers
1	Chemical Properties of Matter	p7	p18
2	Magnets	P20	P31
3	Conservation of Mass and Matter	P33	P44
4	Effects of Forces	P46	P56
5	Electric Circuits	P58	P68
6	Energy Conversion	P70	P80
7	Light	P82	P93
8	Phase Changes and States of Matter	P95	P105

Topic 1 – Chemical Properties of Matter

1.1) What property of matter describes its ability to change into a new substance with different properties?

☐ Physical change

☐ Chemical change

☐ Mass

☐ Density

1.2) Which is an example of a chemical change?

☐ Melting ice

☐ Boiling water

☐ Burning wood

☐ Dissolving sugar in water

1.3) What happens to matter during a chemical change?

☐ It changes color

☐ It changes shape

☐ It forms a new substance

☐ It changes size

1.4) What does the term 'reactivity' refer to in chemistry?

☐ The speed of a chemical reaction

☐ The ability of a substance to undergo a chemical change

☐ The temperature at which a substance changes

☐ The density of a substance

1.5) Which of the following is a sign of a chemical change?

☐ Change in color

☐ Change in shape

☐ Change in phase

☐ Change in size

1.6) What is produced when a chemical change occurs?

☐ A new substance

☐ Heat only

☐ Light only

☐ No new substances

1.7) What is needed to start a chemical reaction?

☐ Reactants

☐ A physical change

☐ A solid form

☐ A liquid form

ALEXANDER-GRACE EDUCATION

1.8) Which of the following is true about a chemical change?

☐ It is easily reversible

☐ It changes the appearance only

☐ It forms new substances with new properties

☐ It does not form new substances

1.9) What is an example of a chemical property?

☐ Color

☐ Shape

☐ Reactivity

☐ Size

1.10) Which is not a sign of a chemical reaction?

☐ Formation of gas

☐ Change in temperature

☐ Change in volume

☐ Change in color

1.11) What is a characteristic of a chemical change?

☐ It cannot be reversed using physical means

☐ It can be reversed by freezing

☐ It only changes the shape of a substance

☐ It only occurs in liquids

1.12) What is the role of heat in a chemical change?

□ It can speed up the reaction

□ It always stops the reaction

□ It does not affect the reaction

□ It only changes the color of substances

1.13) Which of the following is a sign that a chemical change has occurred?

□ Formation of a precipitate

□ Melting of ice

□ Breaking of glass

□ Mixing of two liquids

1.14) What is an indicator of a chemical change in food?

□ Change in taste

□ Change in container size

□ Change in packaging

□ Change in weight

1.15) Which is an example of a substance with a chemical property?

□ Iron rusting

□ Water boiling

□ Ice melting

□ Sugar dissolving

1.16) How does a chemical change differ from a physical change?

☐ It results in new substances

☐ It only changes the state of matter

☐ It is always visible

☐ It is always a fast process

1.17) What happens when a substance reacts with oxygen in a chemical change?

☐ It forms an oxide

☐ It freezes

☐ It evaporates

☐ It melts

1.18) In a chemical reaction, what does the term 'product' refer to?

☐ The substances used in the reaction

☐ The energy released or absorbed

☐ The substances formed as a result of the reaction

☐ The container in which the reaction occurs

1.19) What is necessary for a chemical reaction to occur?

☐ Reactants

☐ A catalyst

☐ Heat

☐ Light

1.20) Which is a characteristic of a chemical reaction?

□ It can be reversed by cooling

□ It involves the exchange of energy

□ It only occurs at high temperatures

□ It does not produce new substances

1.21) What causes iron to rust?

□ Exposure to water and oxygen

□ Freezing temperatures

□ High heat

□ Being in a dark place

1.22) Which is an example of a physical change, not a chemical change?

□ Paper burning

□ Metal rusting

□ Ice melting

□ Wood rotting

1.23) What is the term for a substance that speeds up a chemical reaction without being used up?

□ Catalyst

□ Reactant

□ Product

□ Enzyme

1.24) In a chemical reaction, what is the role of energy?

□ It is always absorbed

□ It is always released

□ It can be either absorbed or released

□ It is not involved

1.25) What is meant by the 'conservation of mass' in a chemical reaction?

□ The total mass of the products is less than the reactants

□ The total mass of the products is more than the reactants

□ The total mass of the products is equal to the mass of the reactants

□ The mass of each product is equal to the mass of each reactant

1.26) Which of the following is a chemical property?

□ Boiling point

□ Density

□ Ability to rust

□ Color

1.27) What is a reactant in a chemical reaction?

□ A substance formed as a result of the reaction

□ A substance that does not change in the reaction

□ A substance that is used up in the reaction

□ The energy required for the reaction

1.28) What happens in a combustion reaction?

☐ A substance combines with oxygen, releasing energy

☐ A substance breaks down into simpler substances

☐ Two substances combine to form a single substance

☐ A solid is formed from two liquids

1.29) What is the role of light in photosynthesis?

☐ It is a reactant

☐ It is a product

☐ It gives the reaction the energy to occur

☐ It is not involved

1.30) How is a new substance identified in a chemical reaction?

☐ By its color change

☐ By its melting point

☐ By its chemical properties

☐ By its size

1.31) What is the main difference between a physical and chemical change?

☐ Physical change alters form, chemical change creates new substances

☐ Physical change is faster than chemical change

☐ Chemical change can be easily reversed

☐ Physical change involves energy release

1.32) Which process is an example of a chemical reaction?

☐ Dissolving salt in water

☐ Freezing water into ice

☐ Digesting food

☐ Cutting paper

1.33) What happens to atoms in a chemical reaction?

☐ They are destroyed

☐ They are created

☐ They are rearranged

☐ They remain the same

1.34) What is a common sign of a chemical change?

☐ A change in color

☐ A change in shape

☐ A change in size

☐ A change in state

1.35) What is necessary for rust to form on iron?

☐ Water and carbon dioxide

☐ Oxygen and carbon dioxide

☐ Water and oxygen

☐ Oxygen and nitrogen

1.36) What type of change is cooking an egg?

☐ Physical change

☐ Chemical change

☐ Both physical and chemical change

☐ Neither physical nor chemical change

1.37) What does pH measure in a substance?

☐ Density

☐ Color

☐ Acidity or basicity

☐ Temperature

1.38) Which of the following is not a chemical reaction?

☐ Baking a cake

☐ Boiling water

☐ Photosynthesis

☐ Rusting of iron

1.39) What is the role of enzymes in chemical reactions?

☐ They slow down reactions

☐ They are not involved in reactions

☐ They speed up reactions

☐ They change the products of reactions

1.40) What is the purpose of photosynthesis?

☐ To provide plants with food

☐ To create leaves

☐ To grow roots

☐ To release water

Topic 1 - Answers

Question Number	Answer	Explanation
1.1	Chemical change	This property describes the ability of matter to form new substances with different properties.
1.2	Burning wood	Burning wood is a chemical change as it results in new substances like ash and smoke.
1.3	It forms a new substance	In a chemical change, the original substance forms a new substance with different properties.
1.4	The ability of a substance to undergo a chemical change	Reactivity refers to how easily a substance undergoes a chemical change.
1.5	Change in color	A change in color is often a sign of a chemical change, indicating new substances are formed.
1.6	A new substance	Chemical changes result in the formation of one or more new substances.
1.7	Reactants	Reactants are the starting substances needed to initiate a chemical reaction.
1.8	It forms new substances with new properties	Chemical changes result in the formation of substances with new properties.
1.9	Reactivity	Reactivity is a chemical property as it describes how a substance chemically reacts with other substances.
1.10	Change in volume	While changes in volume can occur, they are not exclusively indicative of a chemical reaction.
1.11	It cannot be reversed using physical means	Chemical changes are typically irreversible through physical methods.
1.12	It can speed up the reaction	Heat often increases the rate at which chemical reactions occur.
1.13	Formation of a precipitate	The formation of a precipitate is a sign that a new substance has been formed during a chemical reaction.
1.14	Change in taste	A change in taste indicates that a chemical change has occurred in food, altering its composition.
1.15	Iron rusting	Rusting of iron is a chemical property as it involves reacting with oxygen to form rust.
1.16	It results in new substances	Chemical changes result in new substances, unlike physical changes that only alter form or state.
1.17	It forms an oxide	When substances react with oxygen, they typically form oxides.
1.18	The substances formed as a result of the reaction	In a chemical reaction, products are the new substances formed.
1.19	Reactants	Reactants are necessary substances that start a chemical reaction.

1.20	It involves the exchange of energy	Chemical reactions often involve either absorption or release of energy.
1.21	Exposure to water and oxygen	Iron rusts due to its reaction with oxygen and water in the environment.
1.22	Ice melting	Melting ice is a physical change as it only changes the state from solid to liquid.
1.23	Catalyst	A catalyst speeds up a chemical reaction without being consumed in the process.
1.24	It can be either absorbed or released	Energy can either be absorbed or released during a chemical reaction.
1.25	The total mass of the products is equal to the mass of the reactants	According to the law of conservation of mass, the total mass of products equals the mass of reactants in a chemical reaction.
1.26	Ability to rust	The ability to rust is a chemical property, indicating how a substance reacts with oxygen.
1.27	A substance that is used up in the reaction	Reactants are substances that are consumed and transformed during a chemical reaction.
1.28	A substance combines with oxygen, releasing energy	Combustion is a chemical reaction where a substance reacts with oxygen, releasing energy, often as heat.
1.29	It gives the reaction the energy to occur	Light provides the necessary energy for the photosynthesis reaction in plants.
1.30	By its chemical properties	A new substance is identified by its distinct chemical properties after a chemical reaction.
1.31	Physical change alters form, chemical change creates new substances	A physical change alters the form or state of a substance, while a chemical change results in the creation of new substances.
1.32	Digesting food	Digesting food involves breaking down substances into simpler forms, which is a chemical reaction.
1.33	They are rearranged	In a chemical reaction, atoms are rearranged to form new substances.
1.34	A change in color	A change in color can be an indicator of a chemical change, suggesting a reaction has occurred.
1.35	Water and oxygen	Rust forms on iron due to its reaction with water and oxygen.
1.36	Chemical change	Cooking an egg is a chemical change as it results in new substances with different properties.
1.37	Acidity or basicity	pH measures the acidity or basicity of a substance.
1.38	Boiling water	Boiling water is a physical change, not a chemical reaction.
1.39	They speed up reactions	Enzymes are biological catalysts that increase the rate of chemical reactions.
1.40	To provide plants with food	Photosynthesis is the process by which plants produce their own food using sunlight, water, and carbon dioxide.

Topic 2 – Magnets

2.1) What materials are typically attracted to a magnet?

☐ Plastic, wood, glass

☐ Iron, nickel, cobalt

☐ Copper, aluminum, brass

☐ Rubber, clay, paper

2.2) What is the invisible force around a magnet called?

☐ Gravity

☐ Electricity

☐ Magnetic field

☐ Friction

2.3) What are the two ends of a magnet called?

☐ Top and bottom

☐ Left and right

☐ North and south poles

☐ Positive and negative sides

2.4) What happens when you put the north pole of one magnet close to the south pole of another magnet?

☐ They repel each other

☐ They do nothing

☐ They attract each other

☐ They create electricity

2.5) Can a magnet attract an object made of wood?

☐ Yes, always

☐ No, never

☐ Only if it's painted

☐ Only if it's wet

2.6) What happens to a magnet if it is heated to a very high temperature?

☐ It becomes stronger

☐ It becomes weaker or loses its magnetism

☐ It becomes electrically charged

☐ It changes color

2.7) Can the magnetic force pass through materials like paper or plastic?

☐ Yes, always

☐ No, never

☐ Only through paper

☐ Only through plastic

ALEXANDER-GRACE EDUCATION

2.8) What is a temporary magnet?

☐ A magnet that lasts forever

☐ A magnet that loses its magnetism quickly

☐ A magnet that can only attract metal

☐ A magnet that only works in water

2.9) How can you make a magnet weaker?

☐ By freezing it

☐ By dropping it

☐ By heating it

☐ By painting it

2.10) What is the Earth's magnetic field responsible for?

☐ Day and night

☐ Seasons

☐ Protecting the Earth from solar winds

☐ Gravity

2.11) What happens when you put two north poles of magnets close to each other?

☐ They attract each other

☐ They repel each other

☐ They become neutral

☐ They create light

2.12) What is a natural magnet found in the earth called?

☐ Magnetite

☐ Iron

☐ Nickel

☐ Cobalt

2.13) How does a compass work?

☐ Using electricity

☐ Using gravity

☐ Using magnetism

☐ Using light

2.14) What type of magnet can be turned on and off?

☐ Permanent magnet

☐ Temporary magnet

☐ Electromagnet

☐ Natural magnet

2.15) What is the area where a magnet's force can affect objects called?

☐ Magnetic field

☐ Magnetic zone

☐ Magnetic area

☐ Magnetic domain

2.16) Can a magnet attract all types of metal?

☐ Yes, all metals

☐ No, only iron

☐ No, only some types like iron, nickel, and cobalt

☐ Only when heated

2.17) What happens if a magnet is cut in half?

☐ It loses its magnetic properties

☐ Each half becomes a separate magnet

☐ It becomes an electromagnet

☐ It becomes stronger

2.18) What is a magnet that only works when electricity passes through it called?

☐ Permanent magnet

☐ Temporary magnet

☐ Electromagnet

☐ Natural magnet

2.19) What do you call the process of making a material magnetic?

☐ Magnetization

☐ Electrification

☐ Polarization

☐ Activation

2.20) What is a material that does not allow magnetic force to pass through it called?

☐ Conductor

☐ Insulator

☐ Magnetic shield

☐ Non-magnetic material

2.21) What is the strongest part of a magnet?

☐ The middle

☐ The north pole

☐ The edges

☐ The poles

2.22) What is it called when a material temporarily becomes a magnet when placed near a strong magnet?

☐ Magnetization

☐ Polarization

☐ Induction

☐ Activation

2.23) What kind of materials can be magnetized?

☐ All materials

☐ Only metals

☐ Only certain metals like iron, nickel, and cobalt

☐ Only non-metals

2.24) What happens when a magnet is rubbed with a piece of iron?

☐ The iron becomes a permanent magnet

☐ The magnet loses its magnetism

☐ The iron becomes a temporary magnet

☐ Nothing happens

2.25) Can the strength of a magnet's magnetic field be changed?

☐ Yes, by heating or hitting it

☐ No, it always remains the same

☐ Only by using electricity

☐ Only in the presence of another magnet

2.26) What happens when the magnetic fields of two magnets overlap?

☐ They cancel each other out

☐ They create a stronger magnetic field

☐ They create an electric field

☐ They repel each other

2.27) What is a practical use of magnets in everyday life?

☐ In compasses for navigation

☐ In heating water

☐ In creating light

☐ In cooking food

2.28) What is one way to destroy a magnet's magnetism?

☐ By putting it in water

☐ By cutting it

☐ By exposing it to sunlight

☐ By heating it to a high temperature

2.29) What do you call the invisible lines that show the magnetic field of a magnet?

☐ Magnetic waves

☐ Magnetic lines of force

☐ Magnetic rays

☐ Magnetic paths

2.30) How do magnets interact with electric currents?

☐ They have no effect on electric currents

☐ They can create electric currents

☐ They can slow down electric currents

☐ They can change the direction of electric currents

2.31) What is the effect of placing a weak magnet near a strong magnet?

☐ The weak magnet becomes stronger

☐ The weak magnet becomes weaker

☐ The strong magnet becomes weaker

☐ No effect

2.32) Can magnets attract through water?

☐ Yes, always

☐ No, never

☐ Only in saltwater

☐ Only in freshwater

2.33) What happens if you place a magnet near a television or computer screen?

☐ It can damage the screen

☐ It improves the screen's quality

☐ It has no effect

☐ It turns the screen off

2.34) Why do magnets stick to a refrigerator door?

☐ Because of gravity

☐ Because the door is usually made of a magnetic material

☐ Because of static electricity

☐ Because of the paint on the door

2.35) What are electromagnets commonly used for?

☐ In clocks

☐ In refrigerators

☐ In electric generators and motors

☐ In mobile phones

2.36) What is the earth's magnetic field also known as?

□ The solar field

□ The geographic field

□ The geomagnetic field

□ The lunar field

2.37) What is the main difference between a bar magnet and a horseshoe magnet?

□ Their color

□ Their strength

□ Their shape

□ Their material

2.38) What type of magnet can be made by passing electric current through a coil of wire?

□ Permanent magnet

□ Temporary magnet

□ Electromagnet

□ Natural magnet

2.39) What do you call a material that can be attracted to a magnet but does not retain magnetism?

□ Magnetic material

□ Non-magnetic material

□ Temporary magnet

□ Permanent magnet

ALEXANDER-GRACE EDUCATION

2.40) What are the small magnetic regions in a material called?

☐ Magnetic fields

☐ Magnetic poles

☐ Magnetic domains

☐ Magnetic particles

Topic 2 - Answers

Question Number	Answer	Explanation
2.1	Iron, nickel, cobalt	These materials are typically attracted to magnets because of their ferromagnetic properties.
2.2	Magnetic field	The invisible force around a magnet is known as its magnetic field.
2.3	North and south poles	The two ends of a magnet are called the north and south poles.
2.4	They attract each other	The north pole of one magnet attracts the south pole of another magnet.
2.5	No, never	A magnet cannot attract an object made of wood as wood is not a magnetic material.
2.6	It becomes weaker or loses its magnetism	High temperatures can cause a magnet to lose its magnetism.
2.7	Yes, always	Magnetic forces can pass through non-magnetic materials like paper or plastic.
2.8	A magnet that loses its magnetism quickly	A temporary magnet is one that acts like a magnet only when in a magnetic field.
2.9	By heating it	Heating a magnet can weaken it or cause it to lose its magnetism.
2.10	Protecting the Earth from solar winds	The Earth's magnetic field protects the planet from solar winds and cosmic radiation.
2.11	They repel each other	Similar poles of magnets, like two north poles, repel each other.
2.12	Magnetite	Magnetite is a natural magnet found in the earth.
2.13	Using magnetism	A compass works by aligning its magnetic needle with Earth's magnetic field.
2.14	Electromagnet	An electromagnet can be turned on and off with electricity.
2.15	Magnetic field	The area where a magnet's force can affect objects is called its magnetic field.
2.16	No, only some types like iron, nickel, and cobalt	Magnets do not attract all types of metal, only ferromagnetic ones like iron, nickel, and cobalt.
2.17	Each half becomes a separate magnet	When a magnet is cut in half, each piece becomes a separate magnet with its own north and south poles.
2.18	Electromagnet	A magnet that only works when electricity passes through it is called an electromagnet.
2.19	Magnetization	The process of making a material magnetic is called magnetization.

2.20	Magnetic shield	A material that blocks magnetic force is known as a magnetic shield.
2.21	The poles	The strongest part of a magnet is at its poles.
2.22	Induction	When a material becomes a magnet temporarily near a strong magnet, it's known as induction.
2.23	Only certain metals like iron, nickel, and cobalt	Only ferromagnetic materials like iron, nickel, and cobalt can be magnetized.
2.24	The iron becomes a temporary magnet	Rubbing a magnet with iron can temporarily magnetize the iron.
2.25	Yes, by heating or hitting it	The strength of a magnet can change, typically weakening when heated or struck.
2.26	They create a stronger magnetic field	When the magnetic fields of two magnets overlap, they can create a stronger field.
2.27	In compasses for navigation	Magnets are used in compasses for navigation, aligning with the Earth's magnetic field to indicate direction.
2.28	By heating it to a high temperature	Heating a magnet to a high temperature can destroy its magnetism.
2.29	Magnetic lines of force	The invisible lines that represent a magnet's magnetic field are called magnetic lines of force.
2.30	They can create electric currents	Magnets can create electric currents, as seen in electromagnetism and generators.
2.31	The weak magnet becomes stronger	Placing a weak magnet near a strong magnet can temporarily increase the strength of the weak magnet.
2.32	Yes, always	Magnetic forces can attract through water.
2.33	It can damage the screen	Placing a magnet near a screen can cause damage due to the magnet's effect on the screen's magnetic fields.
2.34	Because the door is usually made of a magnetic material	Refrigerator doors are typically made of magnetic materials, allowing magnets to stick to them.
2.35	In electric generators and motors	Electromagnets are commonly used in electric generators and motors.
2.36	The geomagnetic field	Earth's magnetic field is also known as the geomagnetic field.
2.37	Their shape	The main difference between a bar magnet and a horseshoe magnet is their shape.
2.38	Electromagnet	A magnet made by passing electric current through a coil of wire is an electromagnet.
2.39	Temporary magnet	A material that can be attracted to a magnet but does not retain magnetism is a temporary magnet.
2.40	Magnetic domains	The small magnetic regions in a material are called magnetic domains.

Topic 3 – Conservation of Mass and Matter

3.1) What does the law of conservation of mass state?

☐ Mass can be created and destroyed

☐ Mass cannot be created or destroyed

☐ Mass increases in chemical reactions

☐ Mass decreases in chemical reactions

3.2) What happens to the mass of materials in a closed system during a chemical reaction?

☐ It increases

☐ It decreases

☐ It stays the same

☐ It disappears

3.3) In a melting ice cube, what happens to the mass of the water?

☐ It increases

☐ It decreases

☐ It stays the same

☐ It turns into gas

3.4) When wood is burned, what happens to its mass?

□ It vanishes

□ It turns into energy

□ It is conserved in the products of the reaction

□ It increases

3.5) How does the law of conservation of mass apply to everyday cooking?

□ It doesn't apply

□ Mass of ingredients decreases

□ Mass of ingredients increases

□ Mass of ingredients before cooking equals mass after cooking

3.6) When a candle burns, what happens to the wax?

□ It disappears completely

□ It turns into gas and smoke

□ It changes into a different solid

□ It becomes a liquid

3.7) Why does a balloon deflate over time?

□ The air inside turns into another gas

□ The air inside gets absorbed by the balloon

□ The air molecules escape through tiny holes

□ The air inside condenses

3.8) During evaporation, what happens to the mass of the liquid?

☐ It increases

☐ It decreases

☐ It stays the same

☐ It becomes solid

3.9) What is an example of conservation of mass in nature?

☐ Leaves falling from trees

☐ Water cycle

☐ Sun rising and setting

☐ Birds migrating

3.10) In a sealed container, if ice changes to water, what happens to the mass of the container and its contents?

☐ It increases

☐ It decreases

☐ It stays the same

☐ It fluctuates

3.11) When you mix vinegar and baking soda, what happens to the total mass?

☐ It increases

☐ It decreases

☐ It stays the same

☐ It becomes half

3.12) If you freeze water to make ice, does the mass of water change?

▫ Yes, it increases

▫ Yes, it decreases

▫ No, it stays the same

▫ It becomes zero

3.13) In a closed system, if a liquid evaporates, does the mass of the container and liquid change?

▫ Yes, it increases

▫ Yes, it decreases

▫ No, it stays the same

▫ The container's mass increases

3.14) What happens to the mass of a plant as it grows?

▫ It decreases

▫ It stays the same

▫ It increases

▫ It first increases, then decreases

3.15) When ice in a closed container melts, what happens to the level of water?

▫ It increases

▫ It decreases

▫ It stays the same

▫ It disappears

3.16) If you mix two liquids in a closed container, what happens to the total mass?

□ It increases

□ It decreases

□ It stays the same

□ It doubles

3.17) What does conservation of mass mean in a physical change?

□ Mass is lost

□ Mass is gained

□ Total mass remains the same

□ Mass changes into energy

3.18) When salt dissolves in water, what happens to the mass of the solution?

□ It increases

□ It decreases

□ It stays the same

□ The salt's mass disappears

3.19) If you cut a piece of paper into smaller pieces, what happens to its total mass?

□ It increases

□ It decreases

□ It stays the same

□ It becomes half

3.20) When water turns into steam, what happens to its mass?

□ It increases

□ It decreases

□ It stays the same

□ It becomes zero

3.21) What happens to the mass of water when it is boiled in an open pot?

□ It increases

□ It decreases

□ It stays the same

□ It turns into a solid

3.22) If you mix soil and water in a container, what happens to the mass of the mixture?

□ It increases

□ It decreases

□ It stays the same

□ It becomes half

3.23) When making lemonade, what happens to the mass of the ingredients when mixed together?

☐ It increases

☐ It decreases

☐ It stays the same

☐ The mass of water decreases

3.24) In a sealed bag, if an apple rots, what happens to the total mass inside the bag?

☐ It increases

☐ It decreases

☐ It stays the same

☐ It fluctuates

3.25) When you inflate a balloon, what happens to the mass of the balloon and air inside?

☐ It increases

☐ It decreases

☐ It stays the same

☐ The balloon's mass increases

3.26) What happens to the mass of a sugar cube after it dissolves in water?

☐ It increases

☐ It decreases

☐ It stays the same

☐ It disappears

3.27) During the process of photosynthesis, what happens to the mass of a plant?

☐ It decreases

☐ It increases

☐ It stays the same

☐ It becomes half

3.28) If you compress a sponge, what happens to its mass?

☐ It increases

☐ It decreases

☐ It stays the same

☐ It becomes half

3.29) When food is digested, what happens to the mass of the food?

☐ It increases

☐ It decreases

☐ It stays the same

☐ It is completely used up

3.30) What happens to the mass of a candle when it burns?

☐ It increases

☐ It decreases

☐ It stays the same

☐ It fluctuates

3.31) If you paint a wooden block, does the mass of the block change?

☐ Yes, it increases

☐ Yes, it decreases

☐ No, it stays the same

☐ It becomes lighter

3.32) What happens to the mass of water when it is boiled in an open pot?

☐ It increases

☐ It decreases

☐ It stays the same

☐ It becomes steam

3.33) When a plant grows by using water, sunlight, and carbon dioxide, what happens to its mass?

☐ It decreases

☐ It stays the same

☐ It increases

☐ It first increases, then decreases

3.34) Does the mass of a battery change when it is used in a device?

☐ Yes, it increases

☐ Yes, it decreases

☐ No, it stays the same

☐ It becomes zero

3.35) What happens to the mass of a popsicle as it melts?

☐ It increases

☐ It decreases

☐ It stays the same

☐ It becomes water

3.36) If you mix flour and water to make dough, does the total mass change?

☐ Yes, it increases

☐ Yes, it decreases

☐ No, it stays the same

☐ It doubles

3.37) When sugar is heated and caramelizes, what happens to its mass?

☐ It increases

☐ It decreases

☐ It stays the same

☐ It becomes liquid

3.38) In a chemical reaction where gas is released, what happens to the mass of the reactants?

☐ It increases

☐ It decreases

☐ It stays the same

☐ It becomes unpredictable

3.39) Does the mass of a piece of fruit change as it ripens?

☐ Yes, it increases

☐ Yes, it decreases

☐ No, it stays the same

☐ It becomes heavier

3.40) When ice in a sealed bag melts, what happens to the mass of the bag and its contents?

☐ It increases

☐ It decreases

☐ It stays the same

☐ It fluctuates

Topic 3 - Answers

Question Number	Answer	Explanation
3.1	Mass cannot be created or destroyed	The law of conservation of mass states that in a closed system, the mass of substances is conserved, even during chemical reactions.
3.2	It stays the same	In a closed system, the mass of materials remains constant during a chemical reaction.
3.3	It stays the same	The mass of water remains the same when ice melts; only its state changes from solid to liquid.
3.4	It is conserved in the products of the reaction	When wood is burned, its mass is conserved in the products like ash, smoke, and gases.
3.5	Mass of ingredients before cooking equals mass after cooking	In cooking, the total mass of the ingredients remains the same before and after the cooking process, according to the conservation of mass.
3.6	It turns into gas and smoke	When a candle burns, the wax is transformed into gas and smoke, and the mass is conserved in these products.
3.7	The air molecules escape through tiny holes	Over time, air escapes from the balloon through tiny holes, leading to its deflation.
3.8	It stays the same	The mass of a liquid remains the same during evaporation; the liquid just changes to gas.
3.9	Water cycle	The water cycle is an example of conservation of mass in nature, where water changes forms but its total mass remains constant.
3.10	It stays the same	In a sealed container, the mass of the container and its contents remains the same even when ice changes to water.
3.11	It stays the same	When vinegar and baking soda are mixed, the total mass of the mixture remains the same as the mass of the individual components.
3.12	No, it stays the same	The mass of water does not change when it freezes into ice; only its state changes.
3.13	No, it stays the same	In a closed system, the mass of the container and liquid remains the same even if the liquid evaporates.
3.14	It increases	As a plant grows, it absorbs water, carbon dioxide, and nutrients, increasing its mass.
3.15	It stays the same	When ice melts in a closed container, the level of water remains the same as the volume of the ice and water are equal.
3.16	It stays the same	When two liquids are mixed in a closed container, the total mass remains the same.
3.17	Total mass remains the same	In a physical change, the total mass of the material remains the same, as no new substance is formed.
3.18	It increases	When salt dissolves in water, the mass of the solution increases by the mass of the salt added.

3.19	It stays the same	Cutting paper into smaller pieces does not change its total mass; it only changes the size of the pieces.
3.20	It stays the same	When water turns into steam, its mass remains the same, despite the change in state.
3.21	It decreases	When water is boiled in an open pot, some of it evaporates, decreasing its mass.
3.22	It stays the same	Mixing soil and water in a container does not change the total mass of the mixture.
3.23	It stays the same	When lemonade ingredients are mixed, the total mass remains the same as the mass of the individual components.
3.24	It stays the same	In a sealed bag, even if an apple rots, the total mass inside the bag remains constant.
3.25	It increases	When a balloon is inflated, the mass of the balloon and the air inside it increases.
3.26	It stays the same	After a sugar cube dissolves in water, the total mass of the solution remains the same.
3.27	It increases	During photosynthesis, a plant's mass increases as it converts carbon dioxide and water into glucose and oxygen.
3.28	It stays the same	Compressing a sponge changes its volume but not its mass.
3.29	It stays the same	When food is digested, the mass of the food remains the same; it's just converted into different substances.
3.30	It stays the same	When a candle burns, its mass is conserved in the products like melted wax, smoke, and gases.
3.31	Yes, it increases	Painting a wooden block adds the mass of the paint to the block, increasing its total mass.
3.32	It decreases	When water is boiled in an open pot, some of it evaporates, resulting in a decrease in mass.
3.33	It increases	As a plant grows using water, sunlight, and carbon dioxide, its mass increases due to the accumulation of biomass.
3.34	No, it stays the same	The mass of a battery does not change when it is used; only the chemicals inside it change form.
3.35	It stays the same	As a popsicle melts, its mass remains the same, though it changes from solid to liquid.
3.36	No, it stays the same	When flour and water are mixed to make dough, the total mass remains the same as the sum of the individual masses.
3.37	It stays the same	When sugar caramelizes, its mass remains the same despite the change in state and properties.
3.38	It stays the same	In a chemical reaction where gas is released, the mass of the reactants is conserved in the products and the gas.
3.39	It stays the same	The mass of a piece of fruit does not change as it ripens; only its internal composition changes.
3.40	It stays the same	When ice in a sealed bag melts, the total mass of the bag and its contents remains constant

ALEXANDER-GRACE EDUCATION

Topic 4 – Effects of Forces

4.1) What is a force?

☐ A type of energy

☐ A push or pull

☐ A kind of motion

☐ A kind of light

4.2) What happens when two forces act in the same direction?

☐ They cancel each other out

☐ They create a stronger force

☐ They create a weaker force

☐ Nothing happens

4.3) What can forces do to an object?

☐ Change its color

☐ Make it lighter

☐ Change its motion or shape

☐ Make it disappear

4.4) What is gravity?

☐ A force that pushes things upward

☐ A force that exists in space only

☐ A force that pulls objects towards each other

☐ A type of magnetic force

4.5) What happens to the motion of an object if no force is applied to it?

□ It speeds up

□ It slows down

□ It changes direction

□ It stays the same

4.6) How does friction affect the movement of objects?

□ It makes objects move faster

□ It stops objects from moving

□ It changes the direction of movement

□ It slows down or stops movement

4.7) What is an example of a force?

□ Light

□ Heat

□ A magnet pulling on metal

□ Sound

4.8) What effect does pulling have on an object?

□ It pushes the object

□ It stops the object

□ It moves the object towards the force

□ It changes the object's color

4.9) What is the force that opposes motion between two surfaces that are in contact?

□ Gravity

□ Magnetism

□ Friction

□ Electricity

4.10) How can you increase the friction between two surfaces?

□ Paint them

□ Make them wet

□ Make one surface rougher

□ Cool them down

4.11) What is the effect of air resistance on a falling object?

□ It speeds up the fall

□ It has no effect

□ It slows down the fall

□ It changes the direction

4.12) What type of force is used to lift something?

□ Pulling force

□ Pushing force

□ Gravitational force

□ Lifting force

4.13) What happens when you stretch a rubber band?

☐ You apply a pulling force

☐ You apply a pushing force

☐ You reduce gravity

☐ You create friction

4.14) How does the weight of an object affect the force needed to move it?

☐ Lighter objects need more force

☐ Heavier objects need more force

☐ Weight has no effect

☐ All objects need the same force

4.15) What is a balanced force?

☐ When two forces act in opposite directions and are equal

☐ When a single force acts on an object

☐ When two forces cancel each other

☐ When forces cause a change in motion

4.16) What happens to the speed of an object if balanced forces act on it?

☐ It speeds up

☐ It slows down

☐ It changes direction

☐ It stays the same

4.17) What does it mean if an object is in motion?

☐ It is moving

☐ It is at rest

☐ It is heavy

☐ It is light

4.18) What kind of force is needed to change the direction of a moving object?

☐ A stopping force

☐ A gravitational force

☐ A unidirectional force

☐ An unbalanced force

4.19) What effect does oiling the wheels of a bike have?

☐ Increases friction

☐ Decreases friction

☐ Stops the bike

☐ Changes the bike's direction

4.20) How can you show that air has force?

☐ By boiling water

☐ By blowing up a balloon

☐ By cutting paper

☐ By freezing water

4.21) What is the result of unbalanced forces acting on an object?

☐ The object's motion does not change

☐ The object starts moving faster

☐ The object changes its motion

☐ The object becomes heavier

4.22) How does a magnet exert a force?

☐ By pushing objects away

☐ By pulling on certain metals

☐ By increasing gravity

☐ By creating friction

4.23) What happens when you compress a spring?

☐ You apply a lifting force

☐ You reduce friction

☐ You apply a pushing force

☐ You increase gravity

4.24) What is the effect of gravity on objects on Earth?

☐ It pushes them upwards

☐ It pulls them towards the center of the Earth

☐ It makes them lighter

☐ It has no effect

4.25) How do seatbelts in a car use force to keep passengers safe?

☐ By increasing speed

☐ By applying a pulling force

☐ By reducing friction

☐ By providing a stopping force in a collision

4.26) What happens when the forces on an object are balanced?

☐ It moves faster

☐ It moves in a circle

☐ It does not change its motion

☐ It stops moving

4.27) Why does a ball eventually stop rolling on the ground?

☐ Because of gravity

☐ Because of air resistance

☐ Because of magnetism

☐ Because of friction

4.28) How can you increase the force of gravity on an object?

☐ By heating it

☐ By making it larger

☐ By painting it

☐ Gravity's force cannot be increased manually

4.29) What is an example of using force to change the shape of an object?

☐ Heating water

☐ Bending a paperclip

☐ Freezing ice

☐ Breaking glass

4.30) How does a parachute slow down a falling object?

☐ By reducing gravity

☐ By increasing gravity

☐ By increasing air resistance

☐ By applying a magnetic force

4.31) What is the effect of wind on a moving sailboat?

☐ It stops the boat

☐ It changes the boat's direction

☐ It speeds up the boat

☐ It has no effect

4.32) What happens when you twist a bottle cap to open it?

☐ You apply a pulling force

☐ You apply a pushing force

☐ You apply a twisting force

☐ You create friction

4.33) How does a wedge use force to split an object?

☐ By decreasing friction

☐ By increasing weight

☐ By applying a concentrated force

☐ By absorbing energy

4.34) What force causes a ball thrown in the air to come back down?

☐ Magnetic force

☐ Elastic force

☐ Friction

☐ Gravity

4.35) What happens to an object when an applied force is greater than the force of friction?

☐ It stops moving

☐ It does not move

☐ It moves in the direction of the applied force

☐ It moves in the opposite direction

4.36) How does oiling a squeaky door hinge affect the force of friction?

☐ It increases the friction

☐ It decreases the friction

☐ It stops the door from moving

☐ It has no effect

4.37) What type of simple machine is a seesaw?

□ Lever

□ Pulley

□ Wheel and axle

□ Wedge

4.38) How can you make it easier to move a heavy object across the floor?

□ Push it with more force

□ Lift it

□ Use wheels or rollers

□ Use a magnet

4.39) What does a fulcrum do in a lever system?

□ It increases weight

□ It decreases force

□ It provides a pivot point

□ It reduces motion

4.40) Why do objects float in water?

□ Due to magnetic force

□ Due to air resistance

□ Due to the buoyant force

□ Due to gravity

Topic 4 - Answers

Question Number	Answer	Explanation
4.1	A push or pull	A force is an interaction that causes an object to change its motion or shape.
4.2	They create a stronger force	When two forces act in the same direction, they combine to create a stronger force.
4.3	Change its motion or shape	Forces can change the motion or shape of an object by pushing or pulling it.
4.4	A force that pulls objects towards each other	Gravity is the force that pulls objects towards each other, especially noticeable as the attraction towards Earth.
4.5	It stays the same	If no external force is applied to an object, its motion remains constant (Newton's First Law of Motion).
4.6	It slows down or stops movement	Friction is a force that opposes motion, causing objects to slow down or stop.
4.7	A magnet pulling on metal	An example of a force is a magnet exerting a pull on a metallic object.
4.8	It moves the object towards the force	Pulling on an object moves it towards the source of the force.
4.9	Friction	Friction is the force that opposes motion between two surfaces that are touching.
4.10	Make one surface rougher	Increasing the roughness of a surface increases the friction between two surfaces.
4.11	It slows down the fall	Air resistance is a type of friction that acts against the direction of motion, slowing down falling objects.
4.12	Lifting force	Lifting something involves applying a force that moves the object upwards.
4.13	You apply a pulling force	Stretching a rubber band involves applying a force that elongates or pulls the band.
4.14	Heavier objects need more force	The weight of an object affects the amount of force required to move it; heavier objects generally need more force.
4.15	When two forces act in opposite directions and are equal	Balanced forces are equal in size and opposite in direction, leading to no change in motion.
4.16	It stays the same	When balanced forces act on an object, its speed remains constant.
4.17	It is moving	An object is in motion if it is changing its position over time.
4.18	An unbalanced force	Changing the direction of a moving object requires an unbalanced force acting on it.

4.19	Decreases friction	Oiling the wheels of a bike reduces the friction, allowing smoother movement.
4.20	By blowing up a balloon	Demonstrating air has force can be done by blowing up a balloon, which shows air exerting pressure.
4.21	The object changes its motion	Unbalanced forces cause a change in an object's motion, such as starting, stopping, or changing direction.
4.22	By pulling on certain metals	Magnets exert force by attracting certain metals like iron, nickel, and cobalt.
4.23	You apply a pushing force	Compressing a spring involves applying a force that pushes the coils together.
4.24	It pulls them towards the center of the Earth	Gravity pulls objects towards Earth's center, giving them weight and causing them to fall when dropped.
4.25	By providing a stopping force in a collision	Seatbelts apply a force that helps to stop passengers from moving forward in a collision.
4.26	It does not change its motion	When forces on an object are balanced, the object's motion does not change; it either stays at rest or continues to move at the same speed and direction.
4.27	Because of friction	A ball stops rolling on the ground due to friction, which opposes its motion and gradually slows it down.
4.28	Gravity's force cannot be increased manually	The force of gravity on an object cannot be increased by external means; it's a natural force dependent on mass and distance.
4.29	Bending a paperclip	Bending a paperclip is an example of using force to change the shape of an object.
4.30	By increasing air resistance	A parachute slows down a falling object by increasing air resistance, which opposes the downward force of gravity.
4.31	It changes the boat's direction	Wind applies a force on a sailboat's sails, changing its direction or speeding it up.
4.32	You apply a twisting force	Twisting a bottle cap to open it applies a rotational or twisting force.
4.33	By applying a concentrated force	A wedge applies a concentrated force onto a smaller area, making it easier to split or cut an object.
4.34	Gravity	The force of gravity pulls a thrown ball back down to Earth.
4.35	It moves in the direction of the applied force	If the applied force is greater than the force of friction, the object moves in the direction of the applied force.
4.36	It decreases the friction	Oiling a squeaky door hinge reduces the friction, allowing smoother movement of the hinge.
4.37	Lever	A seesaw is an example of a lever, a simple machine that can amplify force.
4.38	Use wheels or rollers	Using wheels or rollers reduces friction, making it easier to move a heavy object across a surface.
4.39	It provides a pivot point	The fulcrum in a lever system provides a pivot point around which the lever rotates.
4.40	Due to the buoyant force	Objects float in water due to the buoyant force, which is the upward force exerted by a fluid that opposes the weight of an immersed object.

Topic 5 – Electric Circuits

5.1) What is an electric circuit?

☐ A path for water flow

☐ A path for heat

☐ A path for electric current

☐ A type of battery

5.2) What are the basic components of a simple electric circuit?

☐ Battery, wire, and a light bulb

☐ Water, wire, and a switch

☐ Solar panel, wire, and a fan

☐ Battery, plastic, and a bulb

5.3) What happens when a circuit is 'open'?

☐ Electricity can flow

☐ Electricity cannot flow

☐ The circuit overheats

☐ It turns into a magnet

5.4) What is the role of a switch in an electric circuit?

☐ It increases the current

☐ It connects the circuit to a light source

☐ It opens or closes the circuit

☐ It reduces the electricity flow

5.5) What does a battery do in a circuit?

□ It cools down the circuit

□ It provides the energy for the circuit

□ It stops the electricity

□ It lights up the bulb

5.6) What material is commonly used to connect the components in a circuit?

□ Plastic

□ Rubber

□ Copper wire

□ Wood

5.7) What happens if you add more bulbs to a simple circuit?

□ The bulbs get brighter

□ The bulbs get dimmer

□ The circuit breaks

□ Nothing changes

5.8) What is a conductor in a circuit?

□ A material that does not allow electricity to pass through

□ A material that allows electricity to pass through easily

□ A part of the battery

□ A part of the bulb

5.9) What is a 'short circuit'?

□ A very small circuit

□ A circuit with a switch

□ A fault in the circuit causing an unintended path

□ A circuit with a battery only

5.10) What is an insulator in the context of electric circuits?

□ A material that allows electricity to flow

□ A material that prevents electricity from flowing

□ A component that generates electricity

□ A component that stores electricity

5.11) What is the purpose of a resistor in a circuit?

□ To speed up the current

□ To store electricity

□ To control the flow of electricity

□ To close the circuit

5.12) What type of circuit allows electricity to flow through more than one path?

□ A simple circuit

□ A parallel circuit

□ A series circuit

□ A closed circuit

5.13) What happens in a series circuit when one bulb burns out?

☐ All bulbs get brighter

☐ All bulbs go out

☐ Other bulbs stay lit

☐ The circuit becomes a parallel circuit

5.14) What does a voltmeter measure in a circuit?

☐ Speed of electricity

☐ Resistance

☐ Electric current

☐ Voltage

5.15) Why are metals good conductors of electricity?

☐ They are flexible

☐ They have insulating properties

☐ They have free electrons

☐ They are strong

5.16) What is the effect of a higher voltage in a circuit?

☐ Decreased current

☐ Increased current

☐ No change in current

☐ Short circuit

5.17) Why is plastic used to cover electrical wires?

□ To make them look nice

□ To conduct electricity

□ To prevent electric shocks

□ To make them stronger

5.18) What happens if you add more batteries to a circuit?

□ Bulbs become dimmer

□ Bulbs become brighter

□ Circuit breaks

□ No change

5.19) What does an ammeter measure in a circuit?

□ Voltage

□ Resistance

□ Electric current

□ Circuit size

5.20) What is a 'closed circuit'?

□ A circuit with no gaps

□ A circuit inside a box

□ A circuit with a switch

□ A circuit with one pathway

5.21) What is the main function of a diode in a circuit?

□ To allow current to flow in one direction only

□ To increase the current

□ To create light

□ To store electricity

5.22) How does a bulb in a circuit light up?

□ By absorbing electricity

□ By reflecting light

□ By converting electrical energy into light

□ By creating heat only

5.23) What is a conductor?

□ A material that does not allow electricity to pass

□ A material that allows electricity to pass easily

□ A type of battery

□ A type of switch

5.24) What is the role of a capacitor in a circuit?

□ To reduce the voltage

□ To store electrical energy

□ To light up the circuit

□ To open the circuit

5.25) How does a fuse protect a circuit?

□ By increasing the current

□ By allowing extra current

□ By breaking the circuit when too much current flows

□ By storing extra current

5.26) What happens when a circuit is overloaded?

□ The current decreases

□ The circuit becomes more efficient

□ Too much current flows, causing potential danger

□ Nothing happens

5.27) Why should water and electricity be kept apart?

□ Water increases the circuit's efficiency

□ Water can cause a short circuit

□ Water acts as a conductor

□ Water lights up the bulb

5.28) What is an insulator?

□ A material that conducts electricity well

□ A material that does not conduct electricity well

□ A component that generates electricity

□ A component that stores electricity

ALEXANDER-GRACE EDUCATION

5.29) What is meant by 'current' in an electric circuit?

☐ The amount of water flowing

☐ The amount of heat generated

☐ The flow of electric charge

☐ The brightness of the bulb

5.30) What can a variable resistor (or rheostat) in a circuit be used to do?

☐ To turn off the circuit

☐ To change the direction of current

☐ To change the resistance and control the current flow

☐ To increase the voltage

5.31) What is the effect of a broken wire in a circuit?

☐ The circuit becomes stronger

☐ The circuit remains the same

☐ The circuit becomes a parallel circuit

☐ The circuit is interrupted and stops working

5.32) How does the size of a wire affect the flow of electricity in a circuit?

☐ Thicker wires decrease the flow

☐ Thicker wires increase the flow

☐ Size does not affect the flow

☐ Only color of the wire affects the flow

5.33) What is the purpose of a relay in a circuit?

☐ To store electricity

☐ To light up the bulb

☐ To control the flow of electricity using an electromagnet

☐ To measure the current

5.34) What happens in a parallel circuit if one component fails?

☐ All components stop working

☐ Other components continue to work

☐ The circuit becomes a series circuit

☐ The current stops flowing

5.35) What is the difference between AC and DC electricity?

☐ AC is safer than DC

☐ DC is used in batteries, AC is used in home outlets

☐ AC can't power electronics

☐ DC flows in two directions

5.36) Why is copper often used for electrical wiring?

☐ Because it's cheap

☐ Because it's a good insulator

☐ Because it's a good conductor of electricity

☐ Because it's strong

5.37) What does LED stand for and what is it used for in circuits?

☐ Light Emitting Diode, used as a light source

☐ Large Electric Device, used as a resistor

☐ Low Energy Design, used for saving energy

☐ Linear Electric Dial, used for measuring voltage

5.38) How does a dimmer switch control the brightness of a light in a circuit?

☐ By changing the color of the light

☐ By turning the light on and off rapidly

☐ By changing the resistance in the circuit

☐ By increasing the voltage

5.39) What is the purpose of a transformer in electrical circuits?

☐ To prevent short circuits

☐ To convert electricity into other forms of energy

☐ To change the voltage of electricity

☐ To store electricity

5.40) How does grounding work in electrical circuits?

☐ By storing excess electricity

☐ By conducting excess electricity safely into the ground

☐ By increasing the circuit's efficiency

☐ By cooling the circuit

Topic 5 - Answers

Question Number	Answer	Explanation
5.1	A path for electric current	An electric circuit provides a path for the flow of electricity.
5.2	Battery, wire, and a light bulb	These are the basic components needed to create a simple circuit.
5.3	Electricity cannot flow	An open circuit means there is a break in the path, preventing electricity from flowing.
5.4	It opens or closes the circuit	A switch controls the flow of electricity by opening (off) or closing (on) the circuit.
5.5	It provides the energy for the circuit	A battery is the source of electrical energy in a circuit.
5.6	Copper wire	Copper wire is commonly used for its good conductivity and flexibility.
5.7	The bulbs get dimmer	Adding more bulbs to a simple circuit increases the resistance, making each bulb dimmer.
5.8	A material that allows electricity to pass through easily	Conductors, like metals, allow electricity to flow through them easily.
5.9	A fault in the circuit causing an unintended path	A short circuit occurs when electricity takes an unintended shortcut, bypassing part of the circuit.
5.10	A material that prevents electricity from flowing	Insulators, such as plastic or rubber, prevent the flow of electricity.
5.11	To control the flow of electricity	A resistor is used to control and limit the flow of electrical current in a circuit.
5.12	A parallel circuit	In parallel circuits, electricity has more than one path to follow.
5.13	All bulbs go out	In a series circuit, if one bulb fails, the entire circuit is broken, and all bulbs go out.
5.14	Voltage	A voltmeter measures the electrical potential difference between two points in a circuit.
5.15	They have free electrons	Metals are good conductors because they have free electrons that facilitate the flow of electricity.
5.16	Increased current	Higher voltage in a circuit typically leads to increased current.
5.17	To prevent electric shocks	Plastic is used as an insulator to cover wires, preventing accidental electric shocks.
5.18	Bulbs become brighter	Adding more batteries increases the voltage, making bulbs in the circuit brighter.

5.19	Electric current	An ammeter measures the amount of electric current flowing through a circuit.
5.20	A circuit with no gaps	A closed circuit is a complete electrical connection around which current flows or circulates.
5.21	To allow current to flow in one direction only	A diode allows current to flow through it in one direction only, acting as a one-way valve for electricity.
5.22	By converting electrical energy into light	A bulb lights up by converting the electrical energy passing through it into light energy.
5.23	A material that allows electricity to pass easily	Conductors, like copper, allow electrical current to flow through them with minimal resistance.
5.24	To store electrical energy	A capacitor stores electrical energy in an electric field, which can be released when needed in the circuit.
5.25	By breaking the circuit when too much current flows	A fuse protects a circuit by breaking the connection if the current becomes too high, preventing damage or fire.
5.26	Too much current flows, causing potential danger	Circuit overload occurs when too much current flows through the wires, which can cause overheating or electrical fires.
5.27	Water can cause a short circuit	Water is a good conductor of electricity; mixing water and electricity can lead to short circuits and is dangerous.
5.28	A material that does not conduct electricity well	Insulators, such as plastic, do not allow electricity to pass through them easily, preventing electrical leaks.
5.29	The flow of electric charge	Electric current is the rate at which electric charge flows through a conductor, like a wire.
5.30	To change the resistance and control the current flow	A variable resistor or rheostat allows the resistance in a circuit to be adjusted, controlling the flow of electric current.
5.31	The circuit is interrupted and stops working	A broken wire interrupts the flow of electricity, causing the circuit to stop working.
5.32	Thicker wires increase the flow	Thicker wires have less resistance, allowing more current to flow through the circuit.
5.33	To control the flow of electricity using an electromagnet	A relay uses an electromagnet to open or close circuits in response to electrical signals.
5.34	Other components continue to work	In a parallel circuit, if one component fails, the other components continue to work because they are on separate paths.
5.35	DC is used in batteries, AC is used in home outlets	Direct Current (DC) is constant and flows in one direction, while Alternating Current (AC) changes direction periodically.
5.36	Because it's a good conductor of electricity	Copper is used for wiring because of its excellent electrical conductivity and flexibility.
5.37	Light Emitting Diode, used as a light source	LEDs (Light Emitting Diodes) are used as energy-efficient light sources in circuits.
5.38	By changing the resistance in the circuit	A dimmer switch controls the brightness of a light by varying the resistance, which adjusts the amount of current flowing to the light.
5.39	To change the voltage of electricity	Transformers are used in electrical circuits to increase or decrease the voltage of electricity.
5.40	By conducting excess electricity safely into the ground	Grounding provides a path for excess electricity to be safely discharged into the ground, reducing the risk of electric shocks.

Topic 6 – Energy Conversion

6.1) What is energy conversion?

☐ Using energy quickly

☐ Storing energy

☐ Changing energy from one form to another

☐ Creating new energy

6.2) What happens in a flashlight to light the bulb?

☐ Chemical energy converts to light energy

☐ Heat energy converts to light energy

☐ Magnetic energy converts to light energy

☐ Electric energy converts to sound energy

6.3) What type of energy does a battery store?

☐ Light energy

☐ Sound energy

☐ Chemical energy

☐ Heat energy

6.4) When you eat food, what type of energy conversion takes place in your body?

☐ Light to sound energy

☐ Chemical to mechanical energy

☐ Heat to light energy

☐ Electric to chemical energy

6.5) What is solar energy converted into by solar panels?

☐ Chemical energy

☐ Sound energy

☐ Heat energy

☐ Electrical energy

6.6) When a car engine burns gasoline, what energy conversion occurs?

☐ Chemical energy to mechanical energy

☐ Mechanical energy to heat energy

☐ Solar energy to chemical energy

☐ Electrical energy to mechanical energy

6.7) What type of energy conversion happens in a windmill?

☐ Chemical to mechanical

☐ Mechanical to electrical

☐ Heat to electrical

☐ Solar to electrical

6.8) How is electricity generated in a hydroelectric power plant?

☐ By burning fuel

☐ By solar panels

☐ By wind turbines

☐ By converting water's kinetic energy to electrical energy

6.9) What happens when a match is lit?

☐ Mechanical energy converts to heat and light energy

☐ Chemical energy converts to heat and light energy

☐ Solar energy converts to heat

☐ Electrical energy converts to light

6.10) How does a microphone work in terms of energy conversion?

☐ Sound energy to light energy

☐ Sound energy to electrical energy

☐ Heat energy to sound energy

☐ Mechanical energy to electrical energy

6.11) What energy conversion occurs in a toaster?

☐ Chemical energy to heat energy

☐ Electrical energy to heat energy

☐ Solar energy to heat energy

☐ Mechanical energy to electrical energy

6.12) How does a plant convert energy?

☐ From electrical to chemical energy

☐ From heat to light energy

☐ From chemical to mechanical energy

☐ From solar to chemical energy (photosynthesis)

6.13) What type of energy conversion takes place when you listen to a radio?

☐ Electrical energy to sound energy

☐ Sound energy to electrical energy

☐ Mechanical energy to sound energy

☐ Chemical energy to electrical energy

6.14) What happens when water evaporates from a pond?

☐ Solar energy converts to heat energy

☐ Heat energy converts to chemical energy

☐ Chemical energy converts to solar energy

☐ Heat energy converts to kinetic energy

6.15) What energy conversion happens in a refrigerator?

☐ Electrical energy to sound energy

☐ Electrical energy to chemical energy

☐ Chemical energy to electrical energy

☐ Electrical energy to heat energy

6.16) What is the energy conversion in a ceiling fan?

☐ Electrical energy to mechanical energy

☐ Mechanical energy to electrical energy

☐ Solar energy to mechanical energy

☐ Chemical energy to mechanical energy

6.17) How is energy converted when you ride a bicycle?

☐ Chemical energy in your body to mechanical energy

☐ Mechanical energy to chemical energy

☐ Solar energy to mechanical energy

☐ Electrical energy to mechanical energy

6.18) What energy conversion occurs in an electric heater?

☐ Chemical to heat energy

☐ Mechanical to heat energy

☐ Electrical to heat energy

☐ Solar to heat energy

6.19) How does a drum convert energy?

☐ Mechanical energy to sound energy

☐ Sound energy to mechanical energy

☐ Electrical energy to sound energy

☐ Chemical energy to sound energy

6.20) What type of energy conversion occurs when ice melts?

☐ Heat energy to chemical energy

☐ Mechanical energy to chemical energy

☐ Chemical energy to heat energy

☐ Heat energy to kinetic energy

6.21) What energy conversion occurs when using a hand-crank flashlight?

☐ Mechanical energy to light energy

☐ Chemical energy to light energy

☐ Solar energy to light energy

☐ Heat energy to light energy

6.22) What happens to the energy in food when animals eat?

☐ It is stored as light energy

☐ It is converted into mechanical and heat energy

☐ It disappears

☐ It turns into sound energy

6.23) How does a thermoelectric generator work?

☐ By converting heat energy to electrical energy

☐ By converting light energy to heat energy

☐ By converting mechanical energy to electrical energy

☐ By converting solar energy to electrical energy

6.24) What energy conversion takes place in a glow stick?

☐ Electrical to light energy

☐ Chemical to light energy

☐ Mechanical to light energy

☐ Heat to light energy

6.25) What happens in a steam engine?

☐ Heat energy is converted to mechanical energy

☐ Solar energy is converted to mechanical energy

☐ Chemical energy is converted to light energy

☐ Mechanical energy is converted to heat energy

6.26) How does a microphone convert sound?

☐ From sound energy to light energy

☐ From sound energy to electrical energy

☐ From mechanical energy to sound energy

☐ From heat energy to sound energy

6.27) What kind of energy conversion occurs in a car engine?

☐ Chemical energy to mechanical energy

☐ Solar energy to mechanical energy

☐ Mechanical energy to heat energy

☐ Electrical energy to mechanical energy

6.28) How does a geothermal power plant generate electricity?

☐ By converting wind energy to electrical energy

☐ By converting solar energy to electrical energy

☐ By converting heat from the Earth to electrical energy

☐ By converting water energy to electrical energy

6.29) What happens when you compress a spring?

☐ Mechanical energy is stored

☐ Chemical energy is released

☐ Electrical energy is created

☐ Heat energy is converted to mechanical energy

6.30) What type of energy conversion happens in an electric kettle?

☐ Electrical energy to heat energy

☐ Chemical energy to heat energy

☐ Mechanical energy to heat energy

☐ Solar energy to heat energy

6.31) What type of energy conversion takes place in a digital watch?

☐ Chemical energy to electrical energy

☐ Mechanical energy to electrical energy

☐ Solar energy to electrical energy

☐ Heat energy to electrical energy

6.32) What energy conversion occurs when brakes are applied to a moving bicycle?

☐ Mechanical energy to heat energy

☐ Mechanical energy to sound energy

☐ Kinetic energy to potential energy

☐ Chemical energy to mechanical energy

6.33) How is energy converted in a hydroelectric dam?

☐ From solar to electrical energy

☐ From kinetic to electrical energy

☐ From mechanical to electrical energy

☐ From heat to electrical energy

6.34) What happens to kinetic energy when a ball is thrown upwards?

☐ It increases

☐ It decreases

☐ It converts into potential energy

☐ It remains the same

6.35) How does a hair dryer convert energy?

☐ From chemical to heat and sound energy

☐ From electrical to heat and sound energy

☐ From solar to heat and sound energy

☐ From mechanical to heat and sound energy

6.36) What energy conversion occurs in a speaker?

☐ Electrical energy to sound energy

☐ Sound energy to electrical energy

☐ Mechanical energy to sound energy

☐ Chemical energy to sound energy

6.37) What energy conversion takes place in a camera flash?

☐ Electrical energy to light energy

☐ Chemical energy to light energy

☐ Mechanical energy to light energy

☐ Solar energy to light energy

6.38) How does a plant convert energy during photosynthesis?

☐ From chemical to solar energy

☐ From mechanical to chemical energy

☐ From solar to chemical energy

☐ From electrical to chemical energy

6.39) What type of energy conversion occurs in a gas stove?

☐ Chemical energy to heat energy

☐ Electrical energy to heat energy

☐ Mechanical energy to heat energy

☐ Solar energy to heat energy

6.40) How does a refrigerator work in terms of energy conversion?

☐ From electrical to mechanical energy

☐ From electrical to chemical energy

☐ From chemical to electrical energy

☐ From electrical to thermal energy

Topic 6 - Answers

Question Number	Answer	Explanation
6.1	Changing energy from one form to another	Energy conversion involves transforming energy from one form to another, like kinetic to potential energy.
6.2	Chemical energy converts to light energy	In a flashlight, the chemical energy stored in the batteries is converted into light energy.
6.3	Chemical energy	Batteries store chemical energy, which can be converted into electrical energy.
6.4	Chemical to mechanical energy	Eating food converts the chemical energy in the food into mechanical energy for the body.
6.5	Electrical energy	Solar panels convert solar energy into electrical energy.
6.6	Chemical energy to mechanical energy	Burning gasoline in a car engine converts chemical energy into mechanical energy to move the car.
6.7	Mechanical to electrical	In windmills, the mechanical energy from the wind is converted into electrical energy.
6.8	By converting water's kinetic energy to electrical energy	Hydroelectric power plants convert the kinetic energy of flowing water into electrical energy.
6.9	Chemical energy converts to heat and light energy	Lighting a match converts chemical energy in the match head into heat and light.
6.10	Sound energy to electrical energy	Microphones convert sound energy into electrical energy for amplification or recording.
6.11	Electrical energy to heat energy	A toaster converts electrical energy into heat energy to toast bread.
6.12	From solar to chemical energy (photosynthesis)	Plants convert solar energy into chemical energy through photosynthesis.
6.13	Electrical energy to sound energy	Radios convert electrical energy into sound energy.
6.14	Heat energy converts to kinetic energy	Evaporation of water from a pond is powered by heat energy, which converts to kinetic energy in the water molecules.
6.15	Electrical energy to heat energy	A refrigerator uses electrical energy and converts it into heat energy (to remove heat from inside).
6.16	Electrical energy to mechanical energy	A ceiling fan converts electrical energy into mechanical energy to spin the blades.
6.17	Chemical energy in your body to mechanical energy	Riding a bicycle converts the chemical energy in your muscles to mechanical energy for movement.
6.18	Electrical to heat energy	An electric heater converts electrical energy into heat energy to warm a space.

6.19	Mechanical energy to sound energy	Playing a drum converts the mechanical energy of the hit into sound energy.
6.20	Heat energy to kinetic energy	Melting ice involves the conversion of heat energy to the kinetic energy of water molecules.
6.21	Mechanical energy to light energy	A hand-crank flashlight converts mechanical energy (from cranking) into light energy.
6.22	It is converted into mechanical and heat energy	The energy in food is converted into mechanical energy for movement and heat energy for body temperature regulation.
6.23	By converting heat energy to electrical energy	Thermoelectric generators convert heat directly into electrical energy through the Seebeck effect.
6.24	Chemical to light energy	Glow sticks use a chemical reaction to produce light without heat.
6.25	Heat energy is converted to mechanical energy	In steam engines, heat energy (from burning coal or other fuel) is converted into mechanical energy.
6.26	From sound energy to electrical energy	Microphones convert sound waves into electrical signals for recording or amplification.
6.27	Chemical energy to mechanical energy	Car engines convert the chemical energy in gasoline into mechanical energy for movement.
6.28	By converting heat from the Earth to electrical energy	Geothermal power plants use heat from the Earth's core to generate electricity.
6.29	Mechanical energy is stored	Compressing a spring stores mechanical energy in the spring.
6.30	Electrical energy to heat energy	An electric kettle converts electrical energy into heat energy to boil water.
6.31	Chemical energy to electrical energy	A digital watch uses a battery to convert chemical energy into electrical energy for its operation.
6.32	Mechanical energy to heat energy	Applying brakes converts the kinetic (mechanical) energy of the bicycle into heat energy.
6.33	From kinetic to electrical energy	Hydroelectric dams convert the kinetic energy of flowing water into electrical energy.
6.34	It converts into potential energy	As the ball is thrown upwards, its kinetic energy decreases and is converted into potential energy.
6.35	From electrical to heat and sound energy	A hair dryer converts electrical energy into heat and sound energy to dry hair.
6.36	Electrical energy to sound energy	Speakers convert electrical signals into sound energy.
6.37	Electrical energy to light energy	A camera flash converts electrical energy into light energy for a brief, intense burst of light.
6.38	From solar to chemical energy	During photosynthesis, plants convert solar energy into chemical energy stored in glucose.
6.39	Chemical energy to heat energy	A gas stove converts the chemical energy of gas into heat energy for cooking.
6.40	From electrical to thermal energy	Refrigerators use electrical energy and convert it into thermal energy to remove heat from inside and keep the contents cold.

ALEXANDER-GRACE EDUCATION

Topic 7 – Light

7.1) What is the main source of light for the Earth?

☐ The Moon

☐ Electric bulbs

☐ The Sun

☐ Fire

7.2) What type of object is a mirror?

☐ Opaque

☐ Translucent

☐ Transparent

☐ Reflective

7.3) What happens when light hits an opaque object?

☐ It passes through

☐ It gets absorbed

☐ It reflects

☐ It disappears

7.4) What is it called when light bends as it passes through a different medium?

☐ Reflection

☐ Absorption

☐ Refraction

☐ Transmission

7.5) Which color is not a part of the visible spectrum?

☐ Purple

☐ Indigo

☐ Black

☐ Green

7.6) What causes a rainbow to appear?

☐ Moonlight

☐ Refraction of sunlight in water droplets

☐ Paint in the sky

☐ Shadows

7.7) What is the speed of light?

☐ 300,000 km/s

☐ 150,000 km/s

☐ 1,000 km/s

☐ 3,000 km/s

7.8) Which of these materials does not allow light to pass through?

□ Glass

□ Water

□ Wood

□ Air

7.9) What type of lens is used in a magnifying glass?

□ Concave

□ Cylindrical

□ Rectangular

□ Convex

7.10) How does light travel?

□ In a straight line

□ In circles

□ Randomly

□ In squares

7.11) What is a shadow?

□ A type of light

□ A reflection

□ A blockage of light

□ A color

7.12) Why can we see ourselves in a mirror?

☐ Because of refraction

☐ Because of dispersion

☐ Because of reflection

☐ Because of absorption

7.13) What does a prism do to white light?

☐ Breaks it into different colors

☐ Stops it

☐ Makes it brighter

☐ Turns it into heat

7.14) What do we need to see an object?

☐ Darkness

☐ A mirror

☐ Light

☐ A lens

7.15) Which is not a natural source of light?

☐ Stars

☐ Fireflies

☐ Candles

☐ The Sun

7.16) What is the effect of a concave lens on light rays?

☐ Straightens them

☐ Scatters them

☐ Bends them inward

☐ Bends them outward

7.17) What is the color spectrum?

☐ A type of rainbow

☐ A painting technique

☐ A single color

☐ All the colors of light mixed together

7.18) What causes an eclipse?

☐ The Earth moving into the Sun's shadow

☐ A star moving in front of the Sun

☐ The Moon moving between the Sun and Earth

☐ A cloud covering the Sun

7.19) What does 'transparent' mean?

☐ Reflects light

☐ Does not let light pass through

☐ Lets light pass through

☐ Scatters light

7.20) What is a light year?

☐ The time it takes light to travel in a year

☐ A type of star

☐ A unit of brightness

☐ The distance light travels in a year

7.21) What type of materials let some light through but not all?

☐ Transparent

☐ Opaque

☐ Translucent

☐ Reflective

7.22) Why does the sky appear blue?

☐ Because of the ocean's reflection

☐ Because of light scattering

☐ Because of pollution

☐ Because it's the color of air

7.23) What happens to light when it passes through a convex lens?

☐ It spreads out

☐ It stops

☐ It bends inward

☐ It bends outward

7.24) What is the phenomenon of splitting white light into its component colors called?

☐ Refraction

☐ Dispersion

☐ Reflection

☐ Absorption

7.25) What is bioluminescence?

☐ Light produced by living organisms

☐ A type of star

☐ A new technology in bulbs

☐ The study of light

7.26) How do our eyes see objects?

☐ By emitting light

☐ By creating images

☐ By reflecting light

☐ By receiving light

7.27) What is the purpose of pupils in our eyes?

☐ To see color

☐ To control the amount of light entering

☐ To see in the dark

☐ To focus images

7.28) Which of the following is an example of artificial light?

☐ Sunlight

☐ Fire

☐ Lightning

☐ Light bulb

7.29) What does luminous mean?

☐ Dark

☐ Shiny

☐ Emitting light

☐ Transparent

7.30) How does the Moon shine?

☐ It produces its own light

☐ It reflects light from the Sun

☐ It absorbs light from stars

☐ It has lightbulbs

7.31) What causes the phenomenon of a 'mirage'?

☐ Reflection of light in water

☐ Refraction of light in the atmosphere

☐ An optical illusion

☐ A special type of shadow

7.32) What is the primary color of light?

☐ Red, Blue, and Green

☐ Red, Yellow, and Blue

☐ Black, White, and Grey

☐ Orange, Purple, and Green

7.33) What is the term for materials that allow no light to pass through?

☐ Transparent

☐ Translucent

☐ Opaque

☐ Reflective

7.34) Why can't we see in the dark?

☐ Because our eyes need rest

☐ Because there is no color

☐ Because there is no light

☐ Because our eyes close automatically

7.35) What is the process of bouncing back of light rays from a surface?

☐ Refraction

☐ Dispersion

☐ Reflection

☐ Absorption

7.36) What kind of image does a plane mirror form?

□ Real and inverted

□ Virtual and inverted

□ Real and upright

□ Virtual and upright

7.37) What is the main difference between a 'laser' light and 'normal' light?

□ Color

□ Brightness

□ Laser light is more focused

□ Laser light is hotter

7.38) What do glasses or contact lenses correct in our eyes?

□ Color blindness

□ The shape of the pupil

□ The bending of light rays

□ The size of the iris

7.39) What type of mirror is used in vehicles to see behind?

□ Plane mirror

□ Convex mirror

□ Concave mirror

□ Transparent mirror

7.40) What happens to light when it enters a denser medium?

☐ It speeds up

☐ It disappears

☐ It bends

☐ It becomes brighter

Topic 7 – Answers

Question Number	Answer	Explanation
7.1	The Sun	The Sun is the main source of light for the Earth.
7.2	Reflective	A mirror is a reflective object.
7.3	It gets absorbed	Light gets absorbed when it hits an opaque object.
7.4	Refraction	Refraction is the bending of light as it passes through a different medium.
7.5	Black	Black is not a part of the visible spectrum; it's the absence of visible light.
7.6	Refraction of sunlight in water droplets	A rainbow is caused by the refraction, reflection, and dispersion of sunlight in water droplets.
7.7	300,000 km/s	The speed of light is approximately 300,000 kilometers per second.
7.8	Wood	Wood is a material that does not allow light to pass through, making it opaque.
7.9	Convex	A magnifying glass typically uses a convex lens.
7.10	In a straight line	Light travels in a straight line.
7.11	A blockage of light	A shadow is created by the blockage of light.
7.12	Because of reflection	We see ourselves in a mirror due to the reflection of light.
7.13	Breaks it into different colors	A prism splits white light into its component colors.
7.14	Light	We need light to see objects.
7.15	Candles	Candles are not a natural source of light but are man-made.
7.16	Bends them outward	A concave lens scatters light rays outward.
7.17	A type of rainbow	The color spectrum includes all the colors that can be produced by visible light.
7.18	The Moon moving between the Sun and Earth	An eclipse is caused when the Moon moves between the Sun and Earth, blocking the sunlight.

7.19	Lets light pass through	Transparent materials allow light to pass through them.
7.20	The distance light travels in a year	A light year is a measure of distance, not time, indicating the distance that light travels in one year.
7.21	Translucent	Translucent materials let some light through but not all.
7.22	Because of light scattering	The sky appears blue due to the scattering of sunlight by the atmosphere.
7.23	It bends inward	A convex lens bends light rays inward.
7.24	Dispersion	Dispersion is the phenomenon of splitting white light into its component colors.
7.25	Light produced by living organisms	Bioluminescence is the production of light by living organisms.
7.26	By receiving light	Our eyes see objects by receiving light that is reflected off these objects.
7.27	To control the amount of light entering	Pupils in our eyes adjust to control the amount of light entering the eye.
7.28	Light bulb	Light bulbs are an example of artificial light.
7.29	Emitting light	Luminous objects are those that emit their own light.
7.30	It reflects light from the Sun	The Moon shines because it reflects light from the Sun.
7.31	Refraction of light in the atmosphere	Mirages are caused by the refraction of light in the atmosphere.
7.32	Red, Blue, and Green	Red, blue, and green are the primary colors of light.
7.33	Opaque	Opaque materials do not allow any light to pass through.
7.34	Because there is no light	We cannot see in the dark because there is no light for our eyes to receive.
7.35	Reflection	Reflection is the process of light bouncing back from a surface.
7.36	Virtual and upright	A plane mirror forms a virtual and upright image.
7.37	Laser light is more focused	Laser light is special because it is highly focused and coherent.
7.38	The bending of light rays	Glasses or contact lenses correct the bending of light rays in our eyes.
7.39	Convex mirror	Vehicles use convex mirrors to see behind.
7.40	It bends	Light bends when it enters a denser medium.

Topic 8 – Phase Changes and States of Matter

8.1) What are the three main states of matter?

☐ Solid, Liquid, Gas

☐ Solid, Gas, Plasma

☐ Liquid, Gas, Plasma

☐ Solid, Liquid, Air

8.2) What is it called when a solid turns into a liquid?

☐ Freezing

☐ Condensation

☐ Evaporation

☐ Melting

8.3) What happens during evaporation?

☐ Liquid turns into a solid

☐ Gas turns into a liquid

☐ Liquid turns into a gas

☐ Solid turns into a gas

8.4) What is condensation?

☐ Turning a gas into a liquid

☐ Turning a liquid into a gas

☐ Turning a solid into a liquid

☐ Turning a liquid into a solid

8.5) What is the process of a liquid becoming a solid?

☐ Melting

☐ Freezing

☐ Evaporation

☐ Condensation

8.6) What is sublimation?

☐ Solid to gas

☐ Gas to solid

☐ Liquid to gas

☐ Gas to liquid

8.7) What state of matter has a definite volume but no definite shape?

☐ Solid

☐ Liquid

☐ Gas

☐ Plasma

8.8) What is the process called when a gas changes directly into a solid?

☐ Sublimation

☐ Deposition

☐ Condensation

☐ Freezing

8.9) In which state of matter do the particles move the fastest?

☐ Solid

☐ Liquid

☐ Gas

☐ Plasma

8.10) What happens to the particles of a substance when it is heated?

☐ They move slower

☐ They get larger

☐ They move faster

☐ They get smaller

8.11) What is the boiling point of water at sea level?

☐ 100 degrees Celsius

☐ 0 degrees Celsius

☐ 50 degrees Celsius

☐ 212 degrees Celsius

8.12) What happens to the particles in a substance during freezing?

☐ They move faster

☐ They stop moving

☐ They move slower

☐ They change shape

8.13) What do we call the change from gas to plasma?

☐ Ionization

☐ Condensation

☐ Freezing

☐ Melting

8.14) What state of matter is characterized by having a definite shape and volume?

☐ Liquid

☐ Gas

☐ Solid

☐ Plasma

8.15) What is the change from a solid to a gas called, skipping the liquid state?

☐ Condensation

☐ Freezing

☐ Sublimation

☐ Deposition

8.16) What happens in the process of condensation?

☐ Particles come together

☐ Particles move apart

☐ Particles stop moving

☐ Particles change shape

8.17) What is the term for the amount of space that matter takes up?

☐ Mass

☐ Volume

☐ Density

☐ Weight

8.18) Which state of matter has particles that are tightly packed and only vibrate in place?

☐ Gas

☐ Liquid

☐ Solid

☐ Plasma

8.19) What state of matter does not have a definite shape but has a definite volume?

☐ Solid

☐ Liquid

☐ Gas

☐ Plasma

8.20) What is it called when a gas turns into a plasma?

☐ Freezing

☐ Condensation

☐ Ionization

☐ Sublimation

8.21) What is created when a gas is cooled and becomes a liquid?

☐ Steam

☐ Dew

☐ Frost

☐ Smoke

8.22) In which state of matter are the particles spaced farthest apart?

☐ Solid

☐ Liquid

☐ Gas

☐ Plasma

8.23) What term describes the change from liquid to solid?

☐ Melting

☐ Evaporation

☐ Freezing

☐ Condensation

8.24) What causes matter to change from one state to another?

☐ Pressure changes

☐ Shape changes

☐ Color changes

☐ Texture changes

8.25) What is the process of a gas turning into a liquid?

□ Melting

□ Freezing

□ Condensation

□ Sublimation

8.26) Which property of matter describes its ability to flow?

□ Rigidity

□ Fluidity

□ Elasticity

□ Plasticity

8.27) What is the name of the temperature at which a liquid turns into a gas?

□ Freezing point

□ Boiling point

□ Condensation point

□ Melting point

8.28) What does the density of an object tell us?

□ Its color

□ Its temperature

□ How much space it takes up

□ How tightly packed its particles are

8.29) When water vapor in the air turns into liquid water on a cold surface, what is this an example of?

☐ Evaporation

☐ Condensation

☐ Sublimation

☐ Deposition

8.30) What happens to water molecules when water freezes?

☐ They move faster

☐ They expand

☐ They contract

☐ They stop moving

8.31) What type of change is boiling water?

☐ Chemical change

☐ Physical change

☐ Biological change

☐ Permanent change

8.32) What is the name given to the change of state from solid to liquid?

☐ Freezing

☐ Condensation

☐ Melting

☐ Vaporization

8.33) What happens to the volume of water when it freezes?

☐ It decreases

☐ It stays the same

☐ It increases

☐ It becomes half

8.34) Which state of matter can fill any shape of container?

☐ Solid

☐ Liquid

☐ Gas

☐ Plasma

8.35) What is the name of the point at which a solid becomes a liquid?

☐ Boiling point

☐ Melting point

☐ Freezing point

☐ Condensation point

8.36) What is the term for a liquid changing into a gas below its boiling point?

☐ Sublimation

☐ Condensation

☐ Evaporation

☐ Deposition

8.37) In what state of matter are particles the least active?

□ Gas

□ Liquid

□ Solid

□ Plasma

8.38) When a gas is changed into a liquid, the process is called?

□ Freezing

□ Melting

□ Condensation

□ Sublimation

8.39) What property of a substance does not change during a phase change?

□ Shape

□ Volume

□ Mass

□ Color

8.40) What process involves heating a liquid to create vapor and then cooling that vapor to create a liquid?

□ Condensation

□ Evaporation

□ Distillation

□ Freezing

Topic 8 – Answers

Question Number	Answer	Explanation
8.1	Solid, Liquid, Gas	These are the three main states of matter: solid (definite shape and volume), liquid (definite volume, no definite shape), and gas (neither definite shape nor volume).
8.2	Melting	Melting is the process where a solid turns into a liquid.
8.3	Liquid turns into a gas	During evaporation, a liquid turns into a gas. This process usually occurs at the surface of the liquid.
8.4	Turning a gas into a liquid	Condensation is the process where a gas turns into a liquid. It typically happens when the gas is cooled down.
8.5	Freezing	Freezing is the process where a liquid becomes a solid. It's the opposite of melting.
8.6	Solid to gas	Sublimation is the transition of a substance directly from the solid to the gas phase without passing through the intermediate liquid phase.
8.7	Liquid	A liquid state of matter has a definite volume but no definite shape, conforming to the shape of its container.
8.8	Deposition	Deposition is the process where a gas changes directly into a solid, bypassing the liquid state.
8.9	Gas	In the gaseous state, particles move the fastest due to the least amount of intermolecular forces acting upon them.
8.10	They move faster	When a substance is heated, its particles move faster due to increased kinetic energy.
8.11	100 degrees Celsius	The boiling point of water at sea level is 100 degrees Celsius or 212 degrees Fahrenheit.
8.12	They move slower	During freezing, particles in a substance move slower as they lose energy and become more closely packed.
8.13	Ionization	The transition from a gas to a plasma involves ionization, where electrons are stripped from gas atoms, creating plasma.
8.14	Solid	A solid state of matter is characterized by having a definite shape and volume. The particles are tightly packed and only vibrate in place.
8.15	Sublimation	Sublimation is the process of a solid changing directly to a gas without first becoming a liquid.
8.16	Particles come together	In condensation, gas particles come together, reducing the distance between them, and form a liquid.
8.17	Volume	Volume is the amount of space that a substance or object occupies or that is enclosed within a container.
8.18	Solid	In a solid state, particles are tightly packed and only vibrate in place. They have a fixed volume and shape.

8.19	Liquid	A liquid state of matter does not have a definite shape but has a definite volume, taking the shape of its container.
8.20	Ionization	When a gas turns into a plasma, it undergoes ionization, where the gas atoms become ionized.
8.21	Dew	When a gas is cooled and becomes a liquid, it forms dew or condensation.
8.22	Gas	In a gaseous state, the particles are spaced the farthest apart compared to solids and liquids.
8.23	Freezing	The change from liquid to solid is known as freezing.
8.24	Temperature and pressure changes	Matter changes from one state to another due to changes in temperature and/or pressure.
8.25	Condensation	The process of a gas turning into a liquid is known as condensation.
8.26	Fluidity	Fluidity describes the ability of a substance to flow, which is a property of liquids and gases.
8.27	Boiling point	The boiling point is the temperature at which a liquid turns into a gas.
8.28	How tightly packed its particles are	Density indicates how tightly packed the particles of a substance are within a given volume.
8.29	Condensation	When water vapor in the air turns into liquid water on a cold surface, it's an example of condensation.
8.30	They expand	When water freezes, its molecules expand, which is why ice is less dense than water.
8.31	Physical change	Boiling water is a physical change as it involves a state change from liquid to gas.
8.32	Melting	The change of state from solid to liquid is known as melting.
8.33	It increases	When water freezes, its volume increases, which is why ice floats on water.
8.34	Gas	Gases can fill any shape of container as their particles move freely and are far apart.
8.35	Melting point	The melting point is the temperature at which a solid becomes a liquid.
8.36	Evaporation	Evaporation is the process where a liquid changes into a gas below its boiling point.
8.37	Solid	In the solid state, particles are the least active as they are tightly packed and only vibrate in place.
8.38	Condensation	When a gas changes into a liquid, the process is called condensation.
8.39	Mass	The mass of a substance does not change during a phase change. It is a conserved property.
8.40	Distillation	Distillation involves heating a liquid to create vapor and then cooling that vapor to create a liquid. It's used for purification.

Ready for More?

The NWEA MAP testing is adaptive. This means that if your student found these questions too tricky or too easy, they may find it useful to practice grades below or above they grade they are in. This will expose students to new concepts and ideas, giving them a better chance at scoring higher in tests.

Alexander-Grace Education produces books covering Mathematics, Sciences, and English, to help your student maximize their potential in these areas.

For errata, please email
alexandergraceeducation@gmail.com

ALEXANDER-GRACE EDUCATION

Made in United States
Troutdale, OR
11/05/2024